FIT MEN WANTED

WANTED

ORIGINAL POSTERS
FROM THE
HOME FRONT

First published in the United Kingdom in 2012 by Thames & Hudson Ltd, 181A High Holborn, London WC1V 7QX

Published in association with Imperial War Museums iwm.org.uk

British Library Cataloguing-in-Publication Data
A catalogue record for this book is available from the British Library

ISBN 978-0-500-29055-2

Printed and bound in China by Toppan Leefung Printing Limited

To find out about all our publications, please visit **www.thamesandhudson.com.** There you can subscribe to our e-newsletter, browse or download our current catalogue, and buy any titles that are in print.

Publisher's note

The caption for each of the detachable posters is given on the reverse side of the image. The name of the organization that originally published each poster is given where it is known.

On the cover: front flap © IWM (PROC 432), © IWM (Art.IWM PST 5076); back flap © IWM (PROC 077), © IWM (PROC 747); back panel © IWM (PROC 019), © IWM (PROC 771), © IWM (Art.IWM PST 4885), © IWM (PROC 076), © IWM (PROC 118), © IWM (Art.IWM PST 6565), © IWM (PROC 775), © IWM (PROC 170), © IWM (Art.IWM PST 7810), © IWM (PROC 772), © IWM (Art.IWM PST 10122), © IWM (PROC 779); inside cover © IWM (PROC 746); © IWM (Art. IWM PST 6062); © IWM (PROC 018); © IWM (PROC 530); © IWM (PROC 568); © IWM (Art. IWM PST 5035); © IWM (PROC 110); © IWM (Art.IWM PST 13720); © IWM (Art.IWM PST 5481); © IWM (Art.IWM PST 11456);); © IWM (PROC 736); © IWM (PROC 003); © IWM (PROC 781); © IWM (PROC 566); © IWM (PROC 745); © IWM (PROC 766); © IWM (PROC 587); © IWM (PROC 125); © IWM (PROC 026); © The Royal Society for the Prevention of Accidents. Image © IWM (PROC 006); © IWM (PROC 776); © The Royal Society for the Prevention of Accidents. Image © IWM (PROC 282); © IWM (PROC 778); © IWM (PROC 390); © IWM (PROC 553); © TfL/ IWM (PROC 090); © IWM (PROC 381); © TfL/ IWM (PROC 174); © IWM (PROC 761)

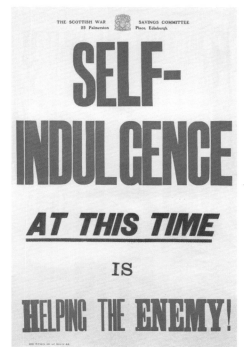

THE POWER OF WORDS

NIGEL STEEL

In the 21st century we live in an ephemeral world. Information. Communication. Invitation. At the push of a button, everything comes — then goes, leaving little behind. The dizzy development of the Internet has upped the pace of life. Few can escape it, no one is beyond reach.

The contrast with the period of the two great wars of the last century could not be starker. Despite the popularity of films and the birth of radio, for the first fifty years of the 20th century communication was still largely through the written or printed word. The number of letters people wrote is almost impossible to comprehend today; they read books in order to learn and be entertained, and it was generally a more literate era. Society prized and understood sophisticated messages delivered through pithy slogans and smart art. This was the heyday of the poster and these striking combinations of words and images stayed on billboards long enough to become one of life's fixtures.

In the years 1914–18 and 1939–45, government, local authorities and other organizations across the United Kingdom used posters and proclamations on an unprecedented scale to drive home their urgent messages to the people. Exhortations of moral duty, calls to action, information and advice, statements of solidarity and mutual resolve: time and again these showed the power of words to motivate and direct a nation in time of war.

The country was fortunate that in both world wars it was able to draw on the skill and experience of a well-established advertising industry. Practitioners used to promoting their products in a competitive market now turned their talents to persuading people to act as the state considered necessary to win a war. They sold a cherished way of life based on the belief that, to endure, the nation needed everyone to act together, that strength would come only through the exercise of shared values and suffering, and that it was unpatriotic not to accept this and not to behave in the common interest.

Only days after the outbreak of the First World War in August 1914 the first call was issued for men to enlist. Within a fortnight the Parliamentary Recruiting Committee had been established to coordinate mass recruitment across the country. Over the course of the next eighteen months, the PRC produced some of the most famous posters of the war. Beginning with quite plain letterpress statements, slowly the PRC developed an irresistibly powerful style that combined high moral values with sharp graphic design.

The poster-driven recruiting campaigns of 1914–18 left a mixed legacy. They showed that incisive messages could successfully reach a wide public if imaginatively and carefully designed. But, as the human cost of the war became more keenly felt, the public also began to resent the hand of government that had reached out to exact such a high price from them. The British people became wary of overt, state-inspired propaganda.

At the start of the Second World War the newly formed Ministry of Information immediately launched a series of rather patronising letterpress posters to steady the nation. The campaign failed, ironically including the now ubiquitous 'Keep Calm and Carry On', and the posters disappeared from sight. The MOI was forced to reassess and look again at the combination of pithy messages and attractive graphics that had worked so well between 1914 and 1916.

From 1940 onwards a new style of poster began to appear. The slogans were cleverer and the images more modern, created by young, avant-garde artists. The posters were peppered with humour, using cartoon images and introducing recognizable 'brand characters'. They rapidly caught the public's imagination and once again, in a distinctive, British way, patriotic propaganda had found its voice.

Viewed from the perspective of the 21st century with its graphics-rich, all-is-possible media, and more than seventy-five years after these posters were issued, many look strange and old fashioned. At the time, they were the cutting edge of public communication. Yet now, imbued with their phlegmatic tone of 'Britain can take it' and 'Business as usual', they are the voice of a distant past. Lifted outside the historical context that explains them, their messages can appear stilted, even wryly amusing. But they also remain strangely comforting. Sometimes we might laugh or sigh at the strangeness of granddad or grandma's jokes, but we remain proud to be the descendants of the people who read and lived these posters.

The posters in this book are mostly 'proclamations', meaning they promulgate direct calls to action. They are not about choice – this product or that one, the red or the blue, the sweet or the sour. They are about telling you what to do. Sometimes the message is shockingly direct. On other occasions it is more subtle, urging people to do the right thing, as if they had a choice. But really the only course is clear. The question remains simply when to act.

Yet they are also very British directives. In the United Kingdom, people generally do not like being told what to do by the state. They retain the right to refuse, unless in so doing they feel they are letting the side down. In many of these posters it is very clear people are being placed under a moral obligation not a legal one. The posters urge you to do it because it is the right thing to do, but they also want you to do it anyway. It is all for the common good.

The posters and proclamations of the two world wars, including all those reproduced here, remain dynamic and powerful reminders of the moral pressures under which the British people lived for ten out of the first forty-five years of the 20th century. Some make you smile, others shock with the directness of their appeal. But every single one makes you stop and think, which is what they were designed to do. After so many years, it is very impressive that they still work.

Nigel Steel
Principal Historian
Imperial War Museums

FAR LEFT AND LEFT Two classic designs from the 1940s that looked beyond the military effort to the equally significant role played by those on the home front.

The trade union leader, Ernest Bevin, was appointed Minister of Labour and National Service in May 1940. Three years later, to boost the number of men working in coal mines, he introduced a scheme to direct a proportion of those being called up into the mines. As a result, 7,000 'Bevin Boys' worked in Britain's mines. Their role in helping to keep this crucial industry going is often forgotten, despite the message of the poster.
© IWM (PROC 110) and © IWM (PROC 015)

National Service Wants You! HMSO

Immediately following the declaration of war of 3 September 1939, the British government introduced a programme of National Service. All men between 18 and 41 had to register and could then be directed into work of national importance; for most this meant being called-up into the armed services. In March 1941, young women aged 20 and 21 also had to register for National Service. This was extended in December to include all women up to the age of 40.

Rally Round the Flag – Every Fit Man Wanted.
Parliamentary Recruiting Committee, 1914

Britain's newly appointed Secretary of State for War, Field Marshal Lord Kitchener, launched his first appeal for 100,000 new troops on 7 August 1914. A second appeal was made on 28 August and three days later the Parliamentary Recruiting Committee was formed to co-ordinate recruitment across the country. The PRC was responsible for many of the war's most memorable posters, and this early appeal used standard patriotic symbols and a simple letterpress design to convey its message.

Say, Young Man! Should You Not Be in Khaki?, 1914

Many of the early recruiting posters of 1914 showed the speed with which they were produced through their loose typesetting and rudimentary design. The simple message of this example was powerfully driven home through a number of key words: 'young man' showed that it was primarily intended to appeal to youth, and 'khaki' was used as an immediately understood shorthand for the army. Its strength lay in its directness.

The Navy Wants Men.
Royal Naval Canadian Volunteer Reserve, pre-1914

The Royal Navy was Britain's Senior Service. The Royal Naval Volunteer Reserve was
established in 1903 to boost the navy's strength by training men to serve in a war
or national emergency. In a show of Imperial solidarity, in May 1914 Canada formed
a Royal Naval Canadian Volunteer Reserve. Once war had started, the RNCVR used
this standard naval recruitment poster, which appeared almost identically in Britain,
to encourage men to enlist in an 'overseas division' and serve in the Royal Navy.

Men of Hull. Get A Move On

By early September 1914, Lord Kitchener's recruiting campaign was reaching its height. Men started to enlist in distinct social groups, joining up together from cities, factories and sports clubs in what became known as 'Pals' battalions. The number of 'Pals' units that a town or city could produce became a matter of civic pride and a reflection of its commitment to the war. Between the beginning of September and end of November, Hull raised four infantry battalions, known as the Hull Commercials, Tradesmen, Sportsmen and T'others.

© IWM (PROC 774)

DO YOU WANT TO BE A CHELSEA DIE-HARD?

IF SO

JOIN THE 17th BATT. MIDDLESEX REGT.

"THE OLD DIE-HARDS"

And follow the lead given by your Favourite Football Players

OFFICES:

FOOTBALL ASSOCIATION, 42, RUSSELL SQUARE, W.C.

WEST AFRICA HOUSE

(KINGSWAY)   or   (Opposite National Theatre)

TOWN HALL, CHELSEA

Issued by the Publicity Department, Central London Recruiting Depot

The Haycock-Cadle Co., Camberwell, S.E.

Do You Want To Be A Chelsea Die-Hard?
Publicity Department, Central London Recruiting Depot, 1914

In 1914, football was enormously popular across Britain, particularly among the working classes. In the initial recruiting campaigns, football and its supporters provided a means of appealing to hundreds of men who might be willing to enlist. Fans were encouraged to show their loyalty to their clubs by joining up. The 1st Football Battalion (formally 17th Battalion, Middlesex Regiment) was set up in December 1914 by William Joynson Hicks, Conservative MP for Brentford. A 2nd Football Battalion followed in June 1915.

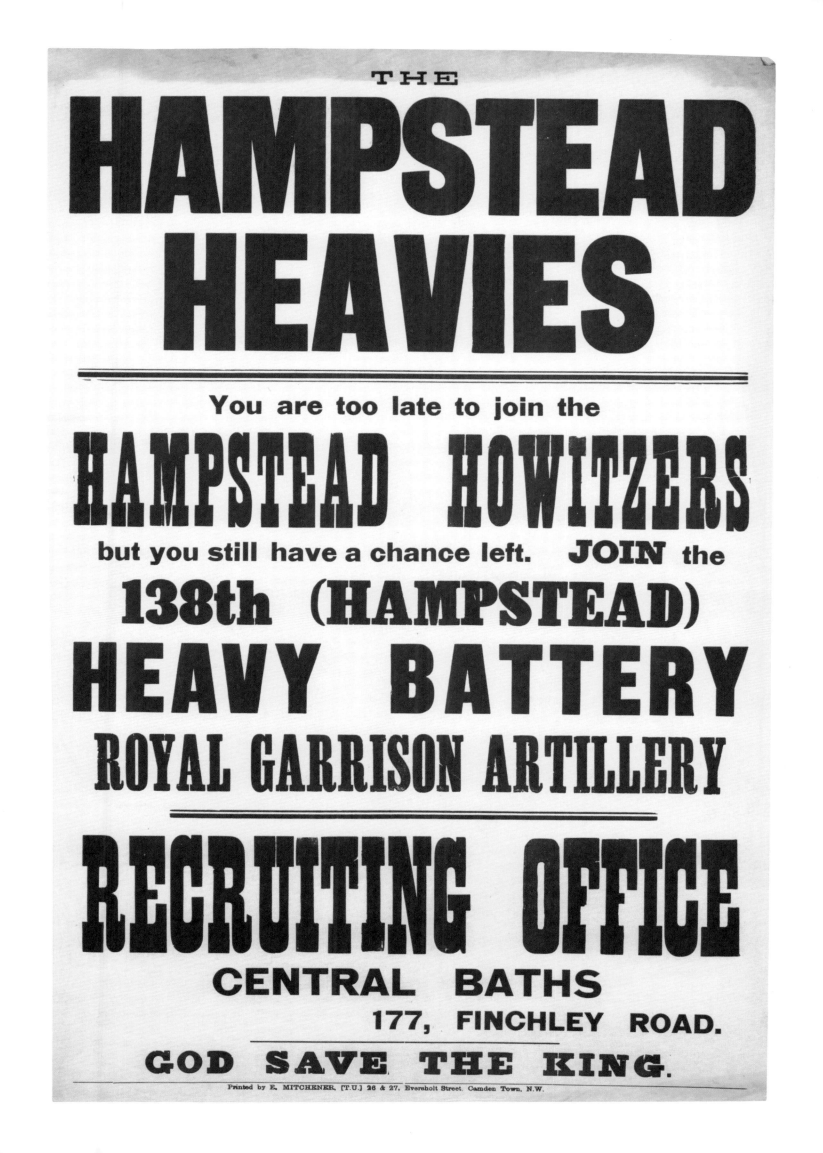

Hampstead Heavies. Royal Garrison Artillery

Many of the smaller communities in Britain were unable to recruit enough men to form full infantry battalions. Instead they raised smaller artillery units. In July 1915, the Mayor of Hampstead agreed to form the 183rd (Howitzer) Brigade. By the autumn it was complete and a new Hampstead artillery battery was started – the Hampstead Heavies. It went to France in April 1916 and served for the rest of the war as the 138th Heavy Battery, Royal Garrison Artillery.

MEN OF ESSEX

DO YOU REMEMBER that the 2nd Battalion of your County Regiment has been at the Front ever since the War began?

DO YOU KNOW that the 1st Battalion has been brought home 6000 miles to take its place in the fighting line?

DO YOU REALIZE that these men are giving their lives to protect your homes from devastation, your wives and daughters from being dishonoured?

Only 52 Essex Men enlisted in the Essex Regiment in the whole month of February.

ARE YOU CONTENT that your County Regiment should fizzle out for want of Essex Men, or would you wish that men from other Counties should fill up its ranks, because Essex Men preferred to stay at home?

This would be a disgrace to Essex.

Your County Regiment has fought in every corner of the Globe, as the honours on its Colours will show you.

THEY MUST HAVE MEN TO REPLACE THEIR CASUALTIES, AND THEY WANT ESSEX MEN.

RALLY ROUND THEIR COLOURS
AND
KEEP THE FLAG FLYING !

Let Women do Women's work, and ESSEX MEN join the ESSEX REGIMENT.

BATTLE HONOURS :

EGYPT,	SALAMANCA,	AVA, ALMA,	NILE 1884-85,
GIBRALTAR, 1779-83,	PENINSULA,	INKERMAN,	SOUTH AFRICA, 1899-02,
HAVANNAH,	BLADENSBURG,	SEVASTOPOL,	RELIEF OF KIMBERLEY,
MORO, BADAJOZ,	WATERLOO,	TAKU FORTS,	PAARDEBERG.

GOD SAVE THE KING.

E. FRENCH & SON, Printers, The Westbury Press, Brentwood.

Men of Essex. Essex Regiment

One of the great strengths of the British army during the First World War was its regimental organization based on cities and counties. This enabled men from different regions of the United Kingdom to feel immediately as if they were part of a long historical tradition. The heroic deeds of their predecessors were used as an ideal for them to live up to. Contrasted here to women's work at home, it was an ongoing story of masculine pride.

© IWM (PROC 386)

Hurry Up! Boys

The University and Public Schools Brigade was a classic 'Pals' unit. The common link its recruits shared was education at one of Britain's leading public schools. At Claridge's Hotel on 27 August 1914 it was resolved to recruit 5,000 public school men. This had been exceeded by mid-September. Four battalions were formed: the 18th, 19th, 20th and 21st Royal Fusiliers. The brigade was renumbered from the 118th to the 98th in 1915.

Special Bantam Battalion. King's Own Royal Lancaster Regiment, 1915

The original minimum height for Kitchener recruits was five foot three (1.6m).
This excluded many men from the industrial north of England. 'Bantam' battalions
for men between five foot and five foot two (1.53 and 1.57m) started to be formed
from November 1914. The following June, the 11th Battalion, King's Own Royal
Lancaster Regiment was formed at Lancaster. It attracted many Lancashire miners.
When it eventually moved to France in June 1916, it included among its ranks the
poet Isaac Rosenberg.

ARE YOU FOND OF CYCLING?
IF SO
WHY NOT CYCLE
FOR THE KING?
RECRUITS WANTED
By the S. Midland Divisional Cyclist Company
(Must be 19, and willing to serve abroad).
CYCLES PROVIDED. Uniform and Clothing issued on enlistment.
Application in person or by letter to
Recruiting Office, 8, Victoria St., Bristol
BAD TEETH NO BAR.

Are You Fond of Cycling? Gloucester Territorial Force Association

The South Midland Division had been formed as part of the army reforms that created the Territorial Force in 1908. It was embodied on the outbreak of the First World War and moved to France in March 1915, where it was numbered the 48th Division. Its units were drawn from the central English shires, including Buckingham, Gloucester, Oxford, Warwick and Worcester. A Divisional Cyclist Company was formed in December 1915, drawing its men from all the existing units as well as new recruits.

PUBLISHED BY THE PARLIAMENTARY RECRUITING COMMITTEE, LONDON. POSTER Nº 103.   PRINTED BY THE ABBEY PRESS, 32 & 34, GREAT PETER STREET, WESTMINSTER, S.W.

THERE ARE THREE TYPES OF MEN

Those who hear the call and obey

Those who delay

And — The Others

TO WHICH DO YOU BELONG?

There are Three Types of Men.
Parliamentary Recruiting Committee, 1915

In placing pressure on men to enlist voluntarily between August 1914 and the introduction of conscription in January 1916, the Parliamentary Recruiting Committee produced over 200 different posters. Most of these relied on 'moral blackmail', stressing the link between duty and conscience and playing on men's senses of guilt and fear of being afraid. Many posters included images; other ones relied on conveying their messages through the simple design of their letterpress.

Men Wanted Now. London Air Raid Debris Clearance Scheme

Before the Second World War, it was widely expected in the United Kingdom that enemy air raids would be devastating, causing severe damage and heavy casualties. Air Raid Precautions (ARP) was established in 1938, but in the end systematic raids on cities did not begin until September 1940. Although fewer people were injured than feared, there was extensive damage to buildings. In London, over a million houses were affected during the Blitz and one in six people were made homeless for at least twenty-four hours.

"It all depends on me"

'It All Depends on Me'

During the Second World War the British government fostered a strong sense of community and mutual strength. The war was a trial borne by the whole country together. Everybody had a part to play and each was as important as the next. Ordinary working men reached out to the people around them. Strength came through being a link in an unbroken chain. The Ministry of Information encapsulated this sense of individual responsibility through the slogan 'It All Depends on Me'.

"It all depends on me"

'It All Depends on Me'

As in the First World War, during the Second World War women across the United Kingdom were drawn into diverse and unfamiliar areas of life. With the Home Front directly under threat, privations were shared equally by both sexes. The government was determined to ensure that everyone knew their effort and sacrifice was fully recognized. The Ministry of Information slogan 'It All Depends on Me' was applied just the same to both men and women. Everybody was shown pulling together.

We Need the Women. Ministry of Labour and National Service

In March 1941, the Ministry of Labour and National Service launched an appeal for more women to volunteer for the services, civil defence and industry. Some 43,000 women had joined up in 1939, but since then the numbers had tailed off. One in four civil defence workers were women and 20,000 had joined the Women's Land Army. But more were needed. Following the introduction of women's conscription, levels rose. By 1944, the size of the WLA, for example, had climbed to 80,000.

To the Women
of Britain.

Some of your men
folk are holding back
on your account

Dont you prove your
love for your Country
by persuading
them to go?

PUBLISHED BY THE PARLIAMENTARY RECRUITING COMMITTEE, LONDON.–POSTER NO. 55   THE ROMWELL PRESS, STRAND, LONDON.

To The Women of Britain. Parliamentary Recruiting Committee, 1915

The Parliamentary Recruiting Committee often used images of women to direct
moral pressure on men to enlist. In this poster from early 1915, the PRC turned
this idea on its head. This time women themselves were the target. It was their
conscience that, hopefully, would be pricked and they who would then work on
their men to join up. Just as it was seen as a man's duty to be a soldier, so it was
a woman's patriotic duty not to hold him back.

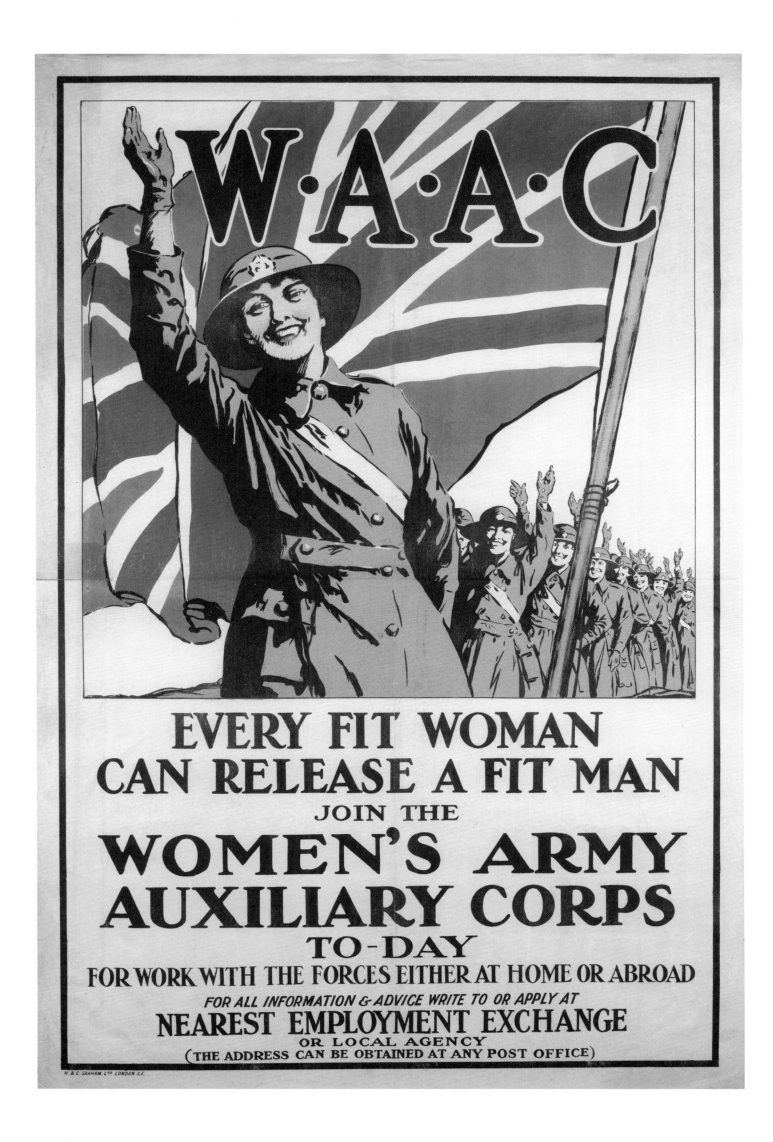

WAAC – Every Fit Woman Can Release A Fit Man.
Women's Army Auxiliary Corps

In 1914 and 1915, several women's organizations were structured along quasi-military lines, such as the Women's Emergency Corps and the Women's Volunteer Reserve. They aimed to release men to fight as soldiers. By 1917, women's military war work needed more formal organization. The Women's Army Auxiliary Corps was established in March. Some 57,000 women went on to serve in the Corps, which was renamed Queen Mary's Army Auxiliary Corps the following year in recognition of the bravery its members showed during the 1918 German offensives.

TRAMWAYS DEPARTMENT.

Good Work
AND
Good Wages
FOR
Good Women

Call at 46 BATH ST.
1O A.M. OR 4 P.M.

ROBERT ANDERSON, PRINTER, GLASGOW.

Good Work and Good Wages for Good Women.
Tramways Department, 1916

Following the outbreak of the First World War, thousands of women sought active
ways to contribute to the war effort. Women had always worked in factories, shops
and on the land, but now they took on a much wider range of jobs. In March 1915,
Glasgow tramways was the first to employ women conductresses and from then the
numbers climbed steadily. The number of women employed in transport eventually
rose from 18,000 in 1914 to 117,000 by 1918.

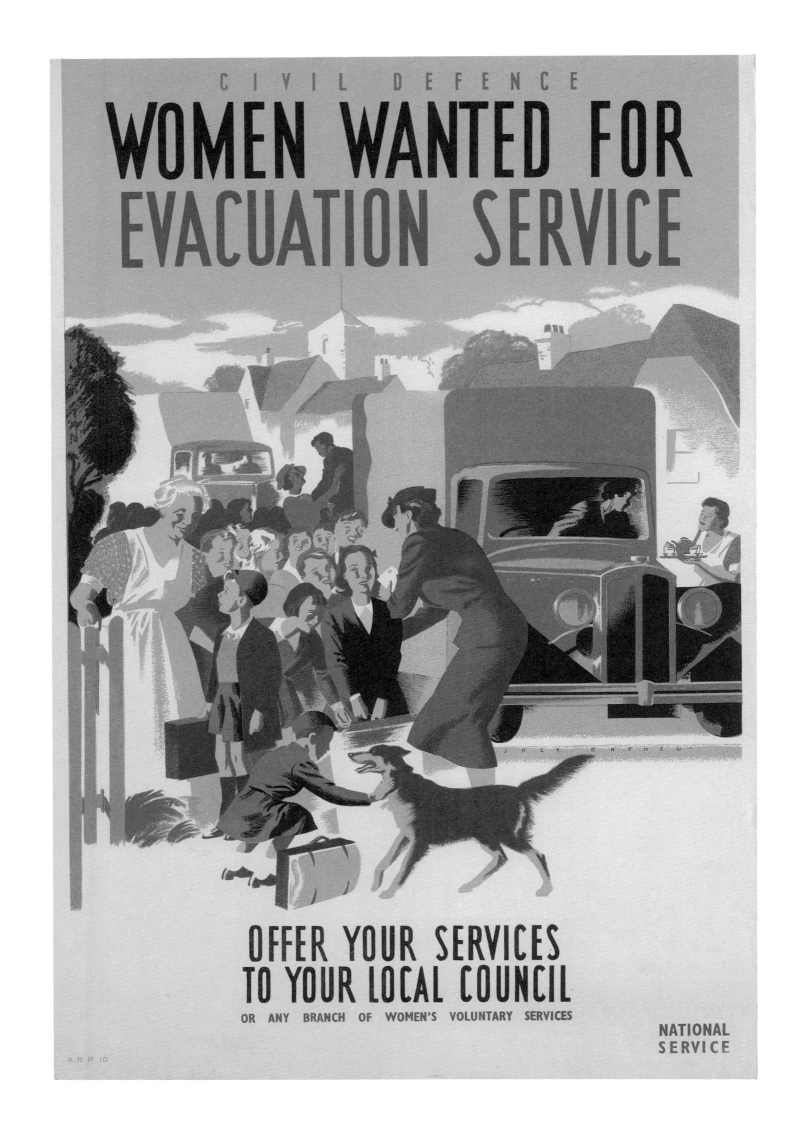

Women Wanted for Evacuation Service. Department of Civil Defence

On 1 September 1939, before war had even been declared, the largest ever
movement of people in Britain began with the evacuation of children, mothers with
small children and the elderly from cities that were expected to be heavily bombed.
Three and a half million vulnerable adults and children were moved to places of
safety, two million privately and and one and a half million by the state. By the end
of September 50 per cent of London's school children had been evacuated and
25 per cent of those living in other large cities.

© IWM (PROC 265)

PLEASE KEEP
YOUR
BEDDING TIDY

String and a Label may be obtained from the Supervisor

THE STRING MUST BE RETURNED

Please Keep Your Bedding Tidy. Department of Civil Defence

In the First World War, air raids on the United Kingdom caused widespread disruption. Often sirens woke people in the night and sent them to their shelters, either public or private, leaving them exhausted in the morning. Destroyed or damaged houses had to be sifted for possessions, and looting was common. Many people, driven from their homes by the raids, took temporary refuge in rest centres. When they did so they took whatever comforts they could carry, such as their own bedding.

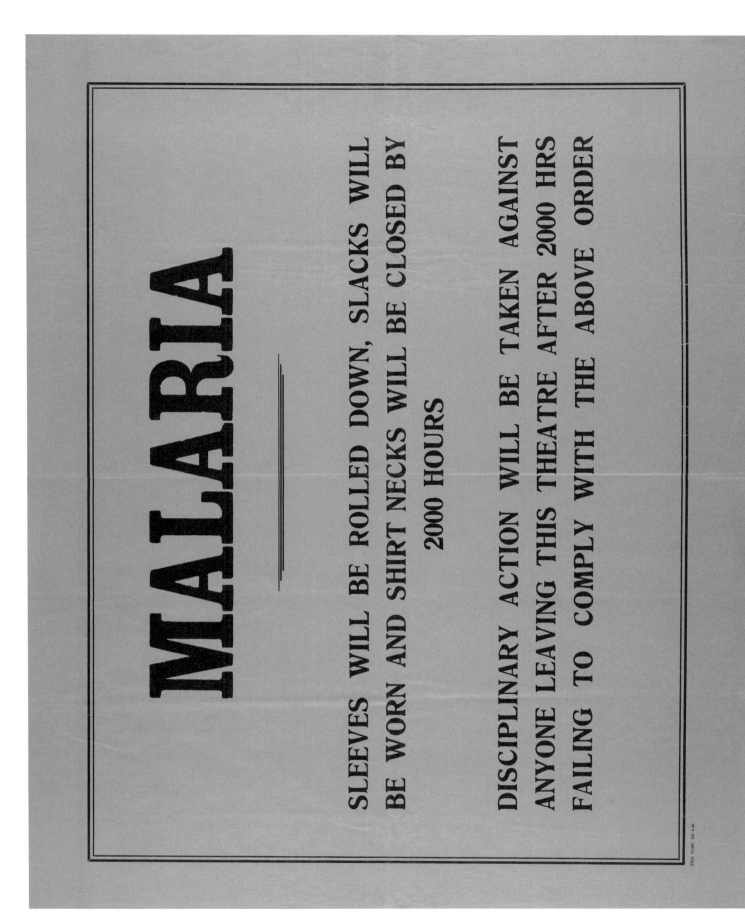

MALARIA

SLEEVES WILL BE ROLLED DOWN, SLACKS WILL BE WORN AND SHIRT NECKS WILL BE CLOSED BY 2000 HOURS

DISCIPLINARY ACTION WILL BE TAKEN AGAINST ANYONE LEAVING THIS THEATRE AFTER 2000 HRS FAILING TO COMPLY WITH THE ABOVE ORDER

Malaria

Wartime losses resulted not only from fighting but also disease. During the Second World War both governments and private institutions (like 'this theatre') sought to increase awareness of how to stop diseases spreading. With colonies to defend in the East, the United Kingdom had soldiers and civilians at risk from the centuries-old killer malaria. When stocks of preventative quinine fell following the Japanese advance across Asia, it became vital to follow other, simple precautions, such as covering limbs to prevent mosquitoes from biting in the first place.

INFLUENZA

PROTECT
YOURSELF

BY GARGLING DAILY

BY REGULAR HABITS

BY FRESH AIR IN
HOME & WORKSHOP

CITY OF COVENTRY
PUBLIC HEALTH DEPARTMENT.

Influenza. City of Coventry Public Health Department

Towards the end of the First World War, a virulent influenza pandemic was
responsible for between fifty and a hundred million deaths worldwide between March
1918 and June 1920. Known as 'Spanish Flu' through its early associations with Spain,
in Britain over a hundred and fifty thousand people died. Fear of a repeat during the
Second World War led many local authorities to encourage the adoption of the kind
of personal hygiene that many believed had helped to contain the earlier outbreak.

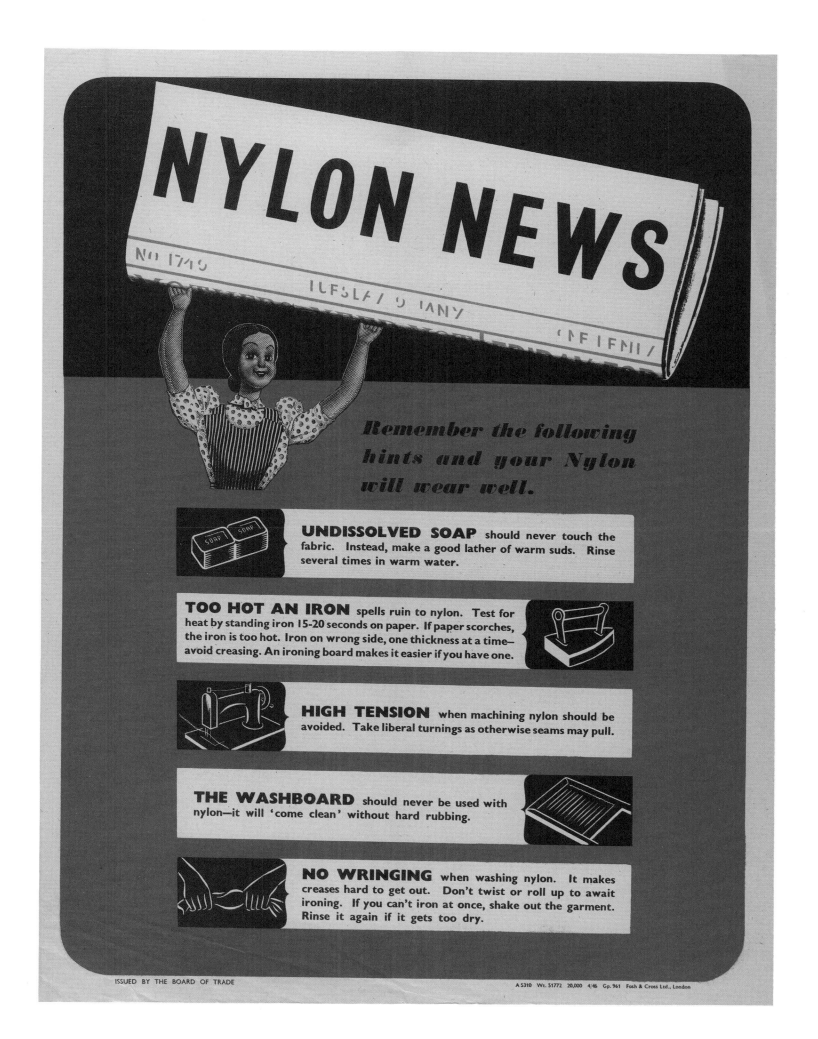

Nylon News. Board of Trade, 1946

In 1939, nylon was a strong, flexible fabric that had only recently been developed in the USA. It was most commonly known through its use in making stockings. The basis of nylon's manufacture was petroleum and in the United Kingdom this quickly became short, leaving 'nylons' highly prized. This 1946 Board of Trade poster, featuring the wartime character Mrs Sew and Sew, was intended to show women how they could make their 'nylons' last and reduce pressure on the country's still limited resources.

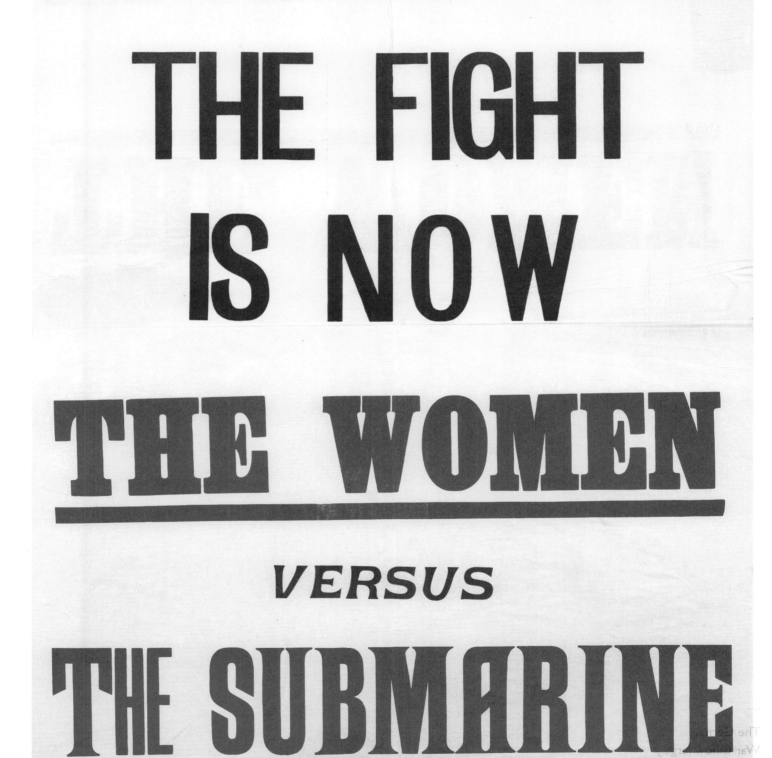

The Fight is Now, The Women Versus The Submarine.
Scottish War Savings Committee, 1917

The German submarine threat against the United Kingdom during the First World
War is now largely forgotten. The Germans launched concerted attempts to
blockade Britain by submarine in 1915, 1916 and 1917. Flour and wheat imports were
particularly hard hit. It became the patriotic duty of housewives, as controllers of the
nation's domestic economy, to make food stocks go a long way. Doing this elevated
the women on the home front to an equal footing with the men on the fighting fronts.

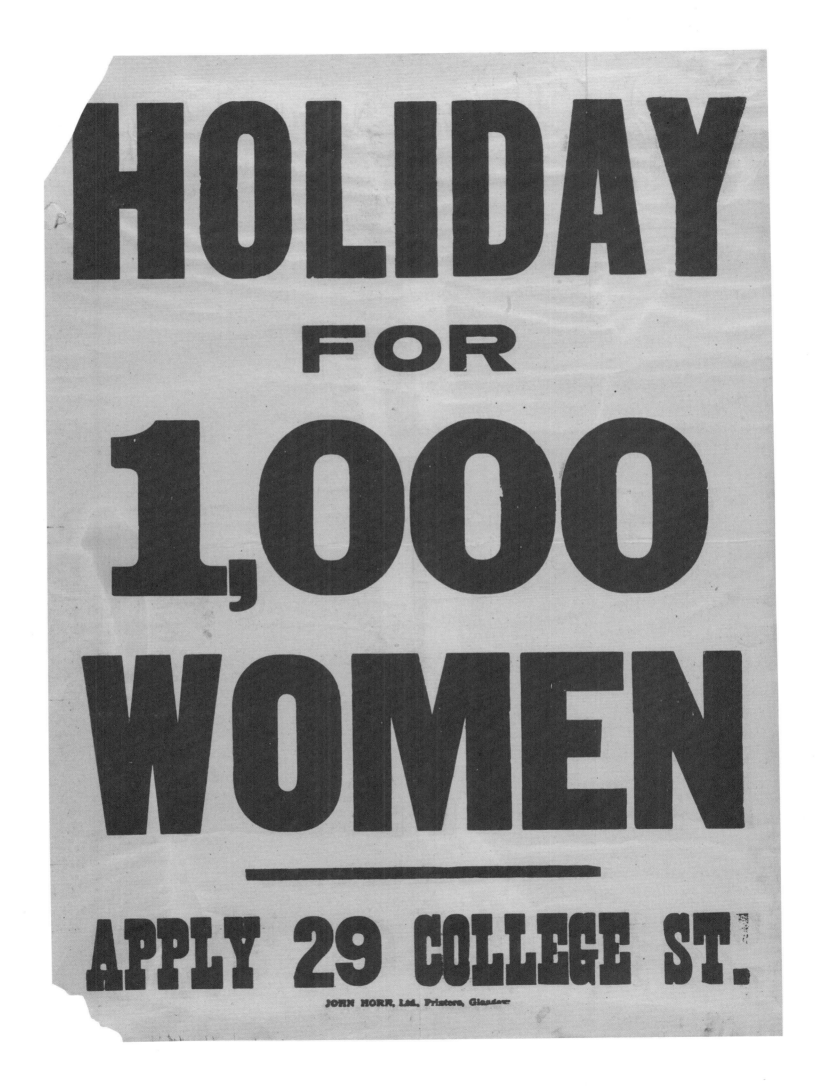

Holiday for 1,000 Women

During the First World War, to encourage more people to work on the land at harvest time, city workers were invited to take 'paid holidays'. They would move to the country during the summer to pick fruit and other crops, getting a break from their regular jobs but still managing to help with the war effort. Using the GPO telephone exchange at 29 College Street as a recruitment office, this poster from Glasgow sought women to go to Auchterarder in Perthshire to pick strawberries and raspberries.

Will you help to win the War?

You can do so by living the open-air life, by working in the fields, by caring for animals and by felling the trees.

M. 106/5.

Will You Help To Win The War? Women's Land Army

As men joined up in 1914 and 1915, more and more women were needed to work on the land to maintain crop yields. Despite the resistance of many farmers, the government's Board of Agriculture and Fisheries began to organize women's land work. In February 1917, it established the Women's Land Army, and its distinctive uniform along with the title 'army' reinforced the vital nature of this area of women's work. Over 16,000 women served in this first Women's Land Army.

© IWM (PROC 783)

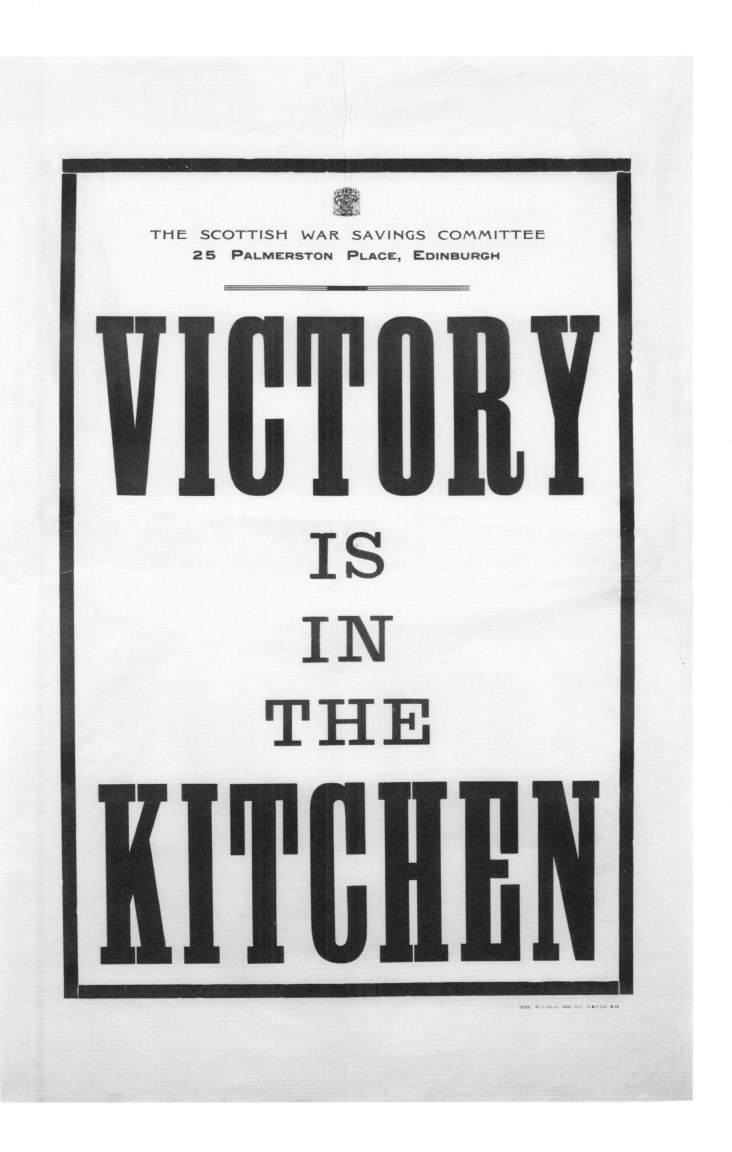

Victory is in the Kitchen. Scottish War Savings Committee, 1917

As the First World War continued, it became increasingly important to maintain the commitment of the home front to the war effort. With their men away at the front and their incomes disrupted, many women were left struggling to make ends meet and keep households running. The increasing shortages of food from the end of 1916 enabled their struggles to be portrayed as of equal importance to the winning of the war as those of the fighting soldiers.

Eat Less Bread. Ministry of Food, 1917

On 2 May 1917, King George V issued a Royal Proclamation calling on people to consume less grain and reduce the volume of bread eaten by one quarter. Those committed to the campaign to 'Eat Less Bread' were encouraged to sign their names on a printed card and hang it in their windows to spur on others. Church ministers were ordered to read the Proclamation to their congregations on the four Sundays that followed the date of its publication.

© IWM (Art.IWM PST 6565)

Don't Waste Bread! Ministry of Food, 1917

Concerns rose towards the end of 1916 about falling stocks of grain and flour as a result of German submarine attacks. As new laws and regulations took hold, people were ordered to eat less bread and flour. In mid-1917 an information campaign claimed forty-eight million slices of bread were being wasted or eaten unnecessarily every day. Over one week this was equivalent to nine shiploads of fresh bread lost. Each slice saved reduced the pressure on merchant ships and helped beat the submarine menace.

© IWM (Art.IWM PST 13354)

All Margarine Sold Here is Government Controlled. Lipton Ltd

By the outbreak of the First World War, margarine had been manufactured for over a hundred years. But its natural colour was white and it remained unpopular on the grounds both of appearance and taste. Food shortages in the United Kingdom, particularly of dairy products and butter, led to an increasing reliance on artificially made margarine. Government regulated both its price and quality. By 1918, it was widely bought and accepted as an alternative to butter.

There is nothing to put in the place of

BEER

—a necessity to the

Strength of Britain

"We've won on Beer before;
We'll win with Beer again."

Beer – a Necessity to the Strength of Britain

Shortages of ingredients led to increasing strains on the production of beer in the United Kingdom during the First World War. Yet drink, and beer in particular, was an integral part of British working men's lives. The volume of beer produced and its strength gradually fell, while the price slowly went up. The proportion of tax also climbed. In 1914, a pint of beer cost 3 pence including a halfpenny tax. By 1918, this had risen to 7 pence including 3½ pence tax.

16092   9¾ x 6½   Grocery

SULTANAS ARE NEWS

PRICES ARE DOWN
DEMAND IS UP...
NATIONAL ADVERTISING
HAS BEGUN...

STOCK & DISPLAY THEM WELL

(36)

676

Sultanas are News

Rationing in the United Kingdom began in January 1940. Using the experience of the First World War, the government introduced a system of control through equal distribution, and more and more food stocks became regulated. To balance the shortage of familiar ingredients, housewives received advice on how to use what was available to boost nutrition and make the unpalatable taste better. This trade advert encouraged retailers to promote the availability of sultanas, often used to improve the flavour of wartime recipes.

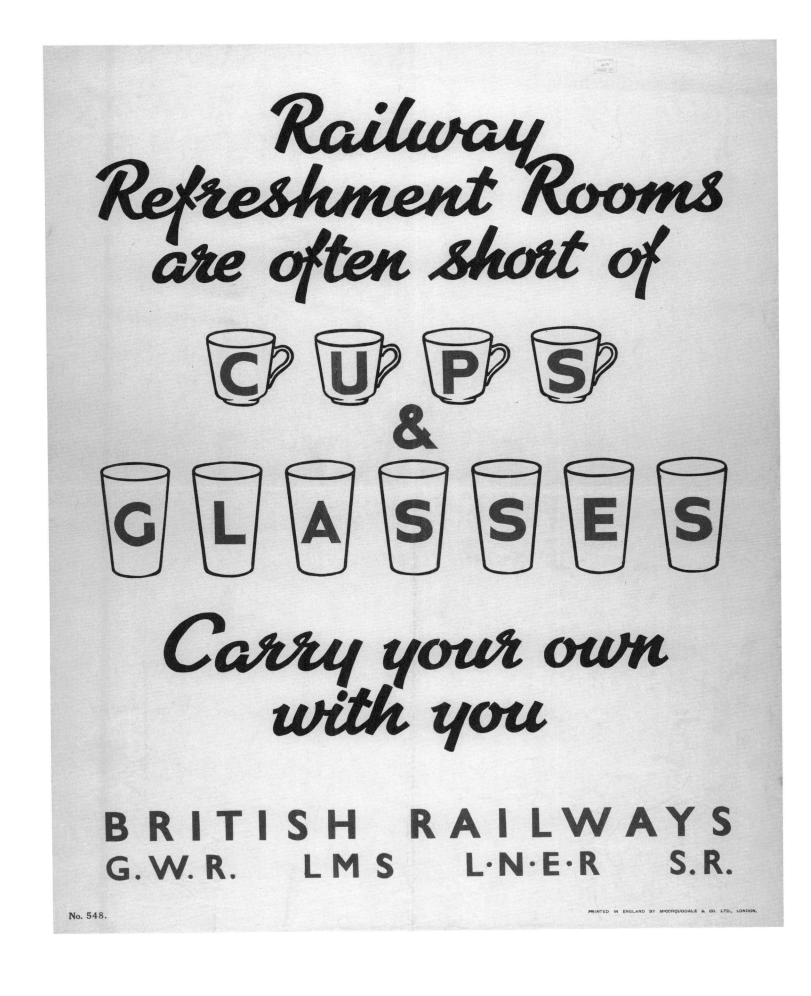

Railway Refreshment Rooms are Often Short of Cups and Glasses.
British Railways

British Railways came into being on 1 January 1948 after the nationalization the previous year of the four major private railway operators in Great Britain: the Great Western Railway (GWR); the London, Midland and Scottish Railway (LMS); the London and North Eastern Railway (LNER); and the Southern Railway (SR). British Railways now ran trains nationwide and, faced by continuing wartime shortages and difficult economic times, from the start found it hard to balance its books.

Housewives. Coventry Transport, 1942

Through the adaptation of its car factories, Coventry became the centre of the aircraft industry in the United Kingdom. Like many other industries, aircraft production underwent rapid expansion. In 1939, the aircraft industry employed 350,000 people and produced 8,000 aircraft. By 1942, this had risen to 1.7 million employees producing 26,000 machines. As elsewhere, in Coventry most workers also undertook voluntary work in the evenings and it was vital that they return home quickly to eat and change before going out again.

LONDON PASSENGER TRANSPORT BOARD

TO ALL ABLE-BODIED MEN

The trains must run to get people to their work and to their homes

The space at the tube stations is limited

Women, children and the infirm need it most

Be a man and leave it to them

55 BROADWAY, S.W.I

To All Able-Bodied Men. London Transport

The impact of bombing on London, particularly during the Blitz between September 1940 and May 1941, was felt particularly badly in transport. Buses, trains and the Underground were all severely hampered after raids, with roads blocked, lines damaged and stations still overrun by those sheltering overnight. To ease pressure on the whole transport system, individual elements such as the London Passenger Transport Board ran campaigns to encourage stronger, fitter passengers, especially men, to walk or cycle.

Man-power, petrol and rubber are released for the war effort when you **carry your shopping home**

Printed for H.M. Stationery Office by Geo. Gibbons Ltd. 51/2359

Carry Your Shopping Home. Ministry of War Transport

The outbreak of war had an immediate effect on the two million private car owners in the United Kingdom. Petrol rationing began within weeks and it became increasingly difficult to keep cars running. Public bus services were also hampered. Shortages of fuel and oil led to 800 buses being taken out of service in London by the end of 1939 and operating hours for bus services were curtailed. Passengers were encouraged to seek other ways of travelling. Many chose to walk.

Rubber is Scarce. Take Care of Your Tyres. Ministry of Supply

Running a car was difficult in the Second World War. Petrol was immediately rationed and the quantity slowly reduced until rationing was suspended completely in July 1942. Vehicles could not easily be serviced, with a Ministry of War Transport certificate needed from November 1941 for spare parts. Most of the United Kingdom's rubber came from Malaya. Shipping it back to make tyres was challenging, even before the Japanese invasion in December 1941. By mid-1942, these factors combined to put most private cars off the road.

It's the little
FUEL SAVINGS

that help to make the
BIG GUNS

Save Coal, Gas,
Electricity, Paraffin—
FUEL for **BATTLE**

It's the little Fuel Savings. Ministry of Fuel and Power, 1939

Petrol rationing began at midnight on 22 September 1939. Car owners were entitled to a monthly allowance ranging from four to ten gallons, depending on their vehicle's size. The ration was gradually reduced, until suspended completely in July 1942. The need to curtail fuel consumption arose less from the difficulty of shipping in supplies than from the voracious demands of aircraft engines. A Lancaster bomber needed 2,000 gallons of petrol just to reach the Ruhr.

This Week and Every Week Salvage is Essential.
Ministry of Supply, 1939

The salvage campaigns of the Second World War were some of the most successful
and effective parts of Britain's war effort. They combined individual patriotism and
zeal, in echoes of the First World War's early recruiting campaigns, with a broad sense
of community and an idealism focused on eliminating waste. The collecting drives
provided many women and children with an opportunity to work directly for the
nation and so to feel a real sense of personal achievement.

These Metals Are Wanted. Ministry of Supply

Although the drive to collect metal to reuse in the aircraft and munitions industries began in January 1940, it was July before it really took hold of the British public's imagination. Radio broadcasts called on women to give up their aluminium cooking pots and utensils. The response was frenzied. At the same time, local authorities and private householders also began to cut down iron railings. Across the nation everyone felt they were doing their bit.

© IWM (PROC 075)

Some Make Big Stuff, Some Make Small. HMSO

From mid-1940 the scale of the campaign to collect metal across the United
Kingdom grew steadily. By May 1942, salvage collectors were bringing in 10,000 tons
per week from some 100,000 households. In April 1943, the overall mass of metal
being salvaged weekly peaked at 110,000 tons. That September a new sweep to
collect aluminium milk-bottle tops claimed enough were being wasted each year to
build fifty Lancaster bombers. By the end of the war around five million tons of metal
had been salvaged.

Join the 'COGS'

The salvage campaigns of the Second World War provided an ideal opportunity to engage and involve children in the war effort. Their sometimes obsessive energy and enthusiasm were harnessed by the government COGS scheme under which children were formed into local salvage collecting groups, often by their schools. There was a COGS song, and badges that reflected the volume of salvage collected. Being a 'COG' showed that you were a vital wheel in the bigger machinery of the war.

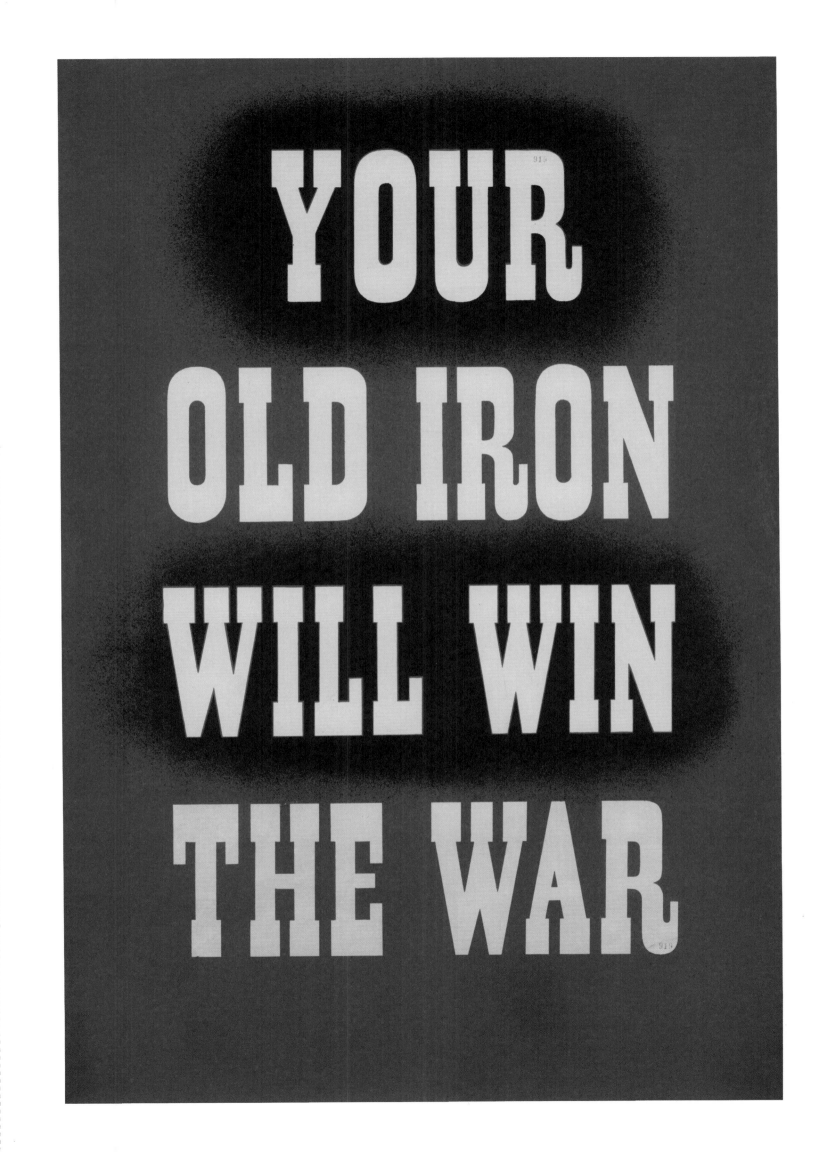

Your Old Iron Will Win the War, 1939

One of the salvage campaigns' most notorious effects was the removal of iron railings from streets and parks. The impact of this can still be seen in the surviving stubs of the railings on many walls in British cities today. By October 1940, 22,000 tons of railings had been voluntarily melted down. A year later a movement was begun to remove compulsorily any still remaining. When the collection of railings finally stopped in September 1944, one million tons had been salvaged.

YOU HAVE A HOUSE

YOUR FRIENDS HAVE A HOUSE

YOU MAY LOSE YOURS

BUT THEY'LL PUT YOU UP FOR A TIME

Arrange now with friends or relatives in another part of the town to go to them if *you* are bombed out—and for *them* to come to you if they are bombed out. Your friends can apply for a temporary lodging allowance if they put you up.

FIX THINGS UP NOW

PRINTED FOR H.M. STATIONERY OFFICE BY FOSH & CROSS LTD., LONDON   (51/1189)

You Have a House

The bombing of British cities was indiscriminate, falling equally on all social classes and causing damage from poor slums to Buckingham Palace. Engendering a strong sense of social cohesion, the war did much to generate a democratic sense of community across the United Kingdom and a widespread desire for life after the war to be more equitable. Almost half a million houses were destroyed and a quarter of a million more badly damaged. Living through this brought people closer together.

Save Kitchen Waste to Feed the Pigs!

The drive not to waste anything during the Second World War led to treating all uneaten food as kitchen waste. The obvious thing to do was feed it to pigs, which would eat almost anything. By 1943, 31,000 tons of food waste was being collected by town councils per month. This provided enough food for 210,000 pigs. Inevitably people became attached to their pigs, and almost 7,000 pig clubs were formed across the country.

From Waste Paper to Munitions of War.
Waste Paper Recovery Association

From a 21st-century perspective, probably the most readily understood area of Second World War salvage is the collection and re-use of paper. A series of posters was published by the Waste Paper Recovery Association to show the many ways in which paper could be re-milled and used again. By the middle of the war, three milllion tons of paper had already been recovered and half the paper and cardboard being produced in the United Kingdom was recycled.

Attack! With your Wastepaper

A wide range of material was sought during the wartime salvage sweeps. Local councils took on responsibility for collecting, much of it through their regular dustbin service, but dedicated bins and collection points were also provided. At various times salvaged material included: metal, paper, kitchen waste, bones, rubber, string, light bulbs, jam jars and glass. One government leaflet explained that if a single 6-inch length of wool was collected from each house it would make 600 sets of army battledress.

Save
WASTE
PAPER
— including wrapping paper, cardboard, cardboard boxes, letters, envelopes, books, newspapers, etc.
You will thus provide raw material for industry and
HELP THE NATIONAL WAR EFFORT
1262

Save Waste Paper

In addition to the collection of paper, the Ministry of Supply launched a Book Drive in 1943 to salvage old books. Fifty-six million volumes were sent in. After careful sorting by librarians, five million were sent out to the recreation centres and messes of the armed forces to supplement those collected in Post Offices during the earlier Books for the Forces campaign. One million were used to replace public library books damaged by the bombing. The rest were pulped to make fresh paper.

"WHEN IN ROME…"

DRINK AS THE ROMANS DRINK!

The **ITALIAN** knows the potency of the local **WINES** and treats them with respect.....

Remember that a **LITRE** of **WINE** contains nearly as much **ALCOHOL** as a **PINT** of **WHISKY**. A glass of vermouth may have greater effect on you than several beers, yet gives no warning of troubles to come.

SOME DRINKS CONTAIN :-
DANGEROUS POISON!
Drink only in
AUTHORISED BARS

P.S.S./B/E 504/K200/3·45

'When in Rome...'. Printing and Stationery Services, 1945

After a difficult and costly advance from southern Italy, Rome was captured by Allied forces on 4 June 1944. Fighting continued northwards until the Germans in Italy surrendered on 2 May 1945. Once Rome was in Allied hands, it became a favoured destination for leave. For many soldiers, being in a foreign country was an experience they had not expected and advice was offered on how to steer round the temptations offered by an attractive but alien culture.

© IWM (PROC 213)

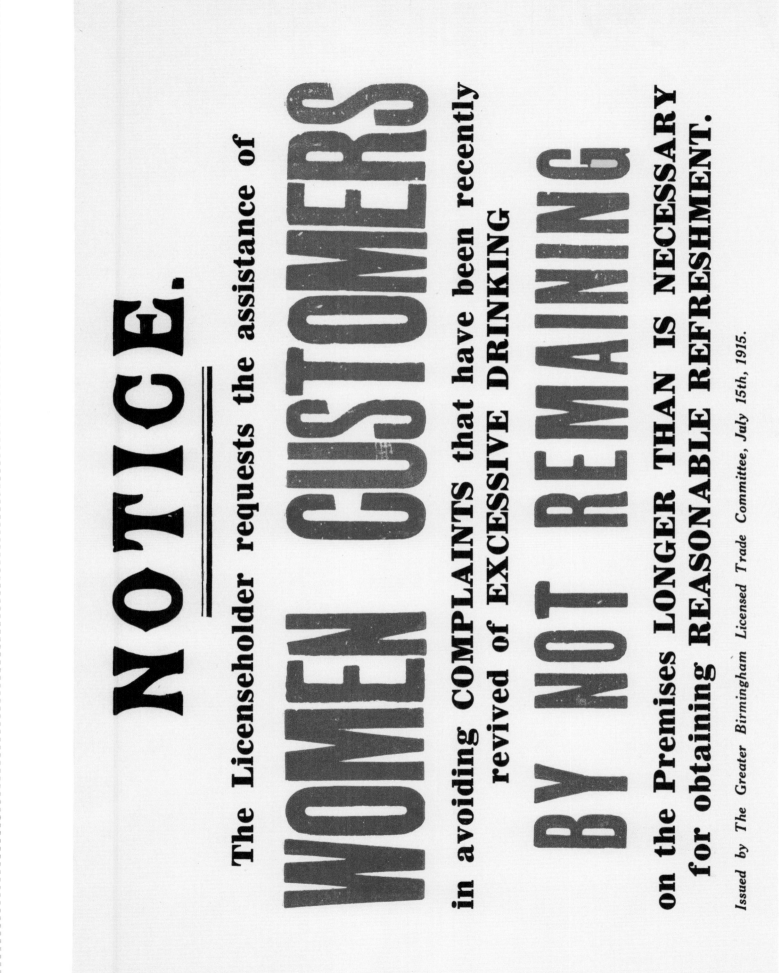

NOTICE.

The Licenseholder requests the assistance of

WOMEN CUSTOMERS

in avoiding COMPLAINTS that have been recently revived of EXCESSIVE DRINKING

BY NOT REMAINING

on the Premises LONGER THAN IS NECESSARY for obtaining REASONABLE REFRESHMENT.

Issued by The Greater Birmingham Licensed Trade Committee, July 15th, 1915.

Notice to Women Customers

In the opening year of the First World War widespread drinking seriously hampered
the level of British industrial production, particularly munitions. In London, pubs
were open from 5 a.m. until after midnight. In 1915, it became illegal to buy drinks for
people in rounds, known as 'treating'. This affected women in particular, as many were
uncomfortable buying their own drinks. However, the regulation of drinking slowly
took effect, with weekly convictions for drunkenness in England and Wales falling
from 3,300 in 1914 to 440 in 1918.

Don't Take Alcoholic Drinks on MONDAYS.

In view of the great sacrifices freely made by our sailors and soldiers, the National Organizing Committee feels sure that all who remain at home will willingly help the Country in this way.

PUBLISHED BY THE NATIONAL ORGANIZING COMMITTEE FOR WAR SAVINGS, LONDON.

PRINTED BY ROBERTS & LEETE. LTD. LONDON.

Don't Take Alcoholic Drinks on Mondays.
The National Organizing Committee for War Savings, 1916

During the First World War, to combat heavy drinking by industrial workers in the
United Kingdom, new laws and regulations were introduced from 1915 onwards. The
government established the Central Control Board to control the sale of alcohol and
opening hours of licensed premises in certain areas. By March 1916, these affected
twenty-seven regions and thirty million people. At the end of the war opening hours
were restricted across most of the country, establishing a pattern still familiar today.

"WE ARE FIGHTING
GERMANY, AUSTRIA,
AND DRINK; AND, AS
FAR AS I CAN SEE,
THE GREATEST OF
THESE THREE DEADLY
FOES IS DRINK."

THE RIGHT HON. D. LLOYD GEORGE.

March 29th, 1915.

Issued by the Temperance Department of the Wesleyan Methodist Church, Tothill Street, Westminster, S.W.

'We Are Fighting Germany, Austria and Drink'. The Temperance
Department of the Wesleyan Methodist Church, 1915

In 1915, the Chancellor of the Exchequer, David Lloyd George, was a well-known
supporter of the Temperance movement in Britain. In speeches in February and
March 1915, Lloyd George claimed that heavy drinking was causing severe damage
to the wartime economy and called for tighter restrictions. King George V announced
that he was giving up alcohol for the duration of the war. He later claimed Lloyd
George had tricked him into 'taking the pledge'.

© IWM (Art.IWM PST 13358)

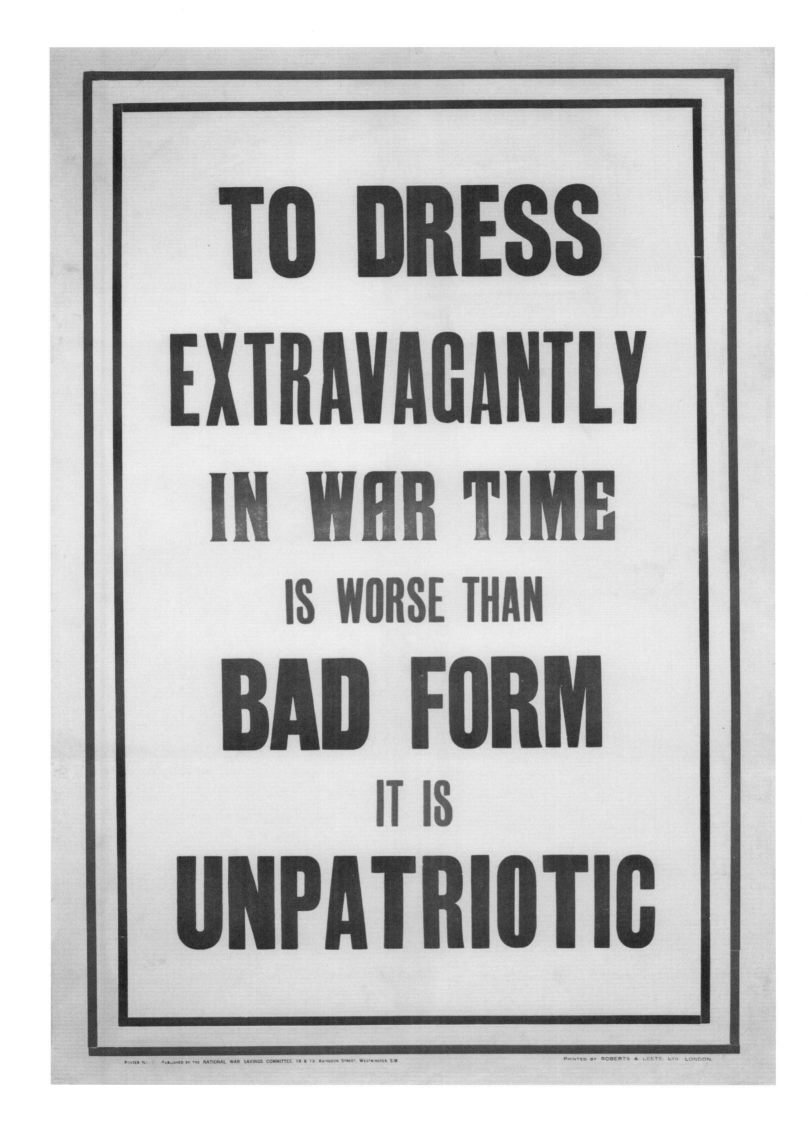

To Dress Extravagantly in War Time.
The National War Savings Committee, 1916

By 1916, most people across the United Kingdom were feeling the pinch of the war.
Shortages of many materials escalated and economy was promoted everywhere.
At the same time, more and more women took on war work and experienced a
significant rise in their incomes compared to the pre-war world. Just because it was
wartime, fashion lost none of its allure. To prevent waste and ostentation, extravagance
was presented as morally unacceptable. Patriotic people dressed considerately.

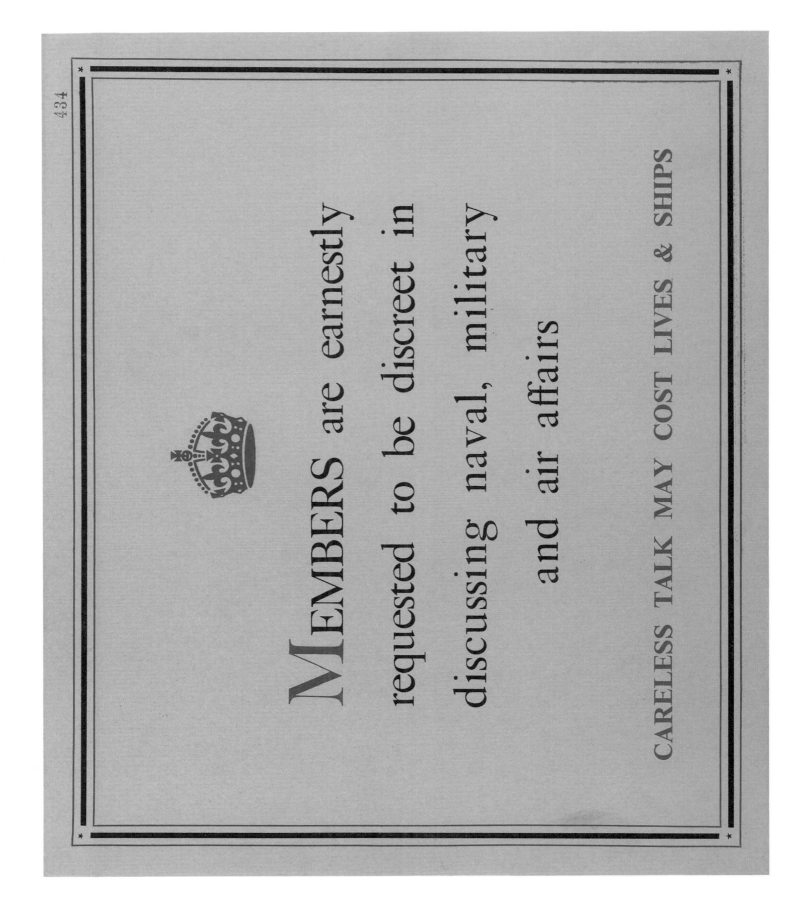

434

MEMBERS are earnestly requested to be discreet in discussing naval, military and air affairs

CARELESS TALK MAY COST LIVES & SHIPS

Careless Talk May Cost Lives and Ships

Beginning in 1940, Britain's Ministry of Information initiated a long-running campaign against false rumours and the indiscreet discussion of war news. Built around one of the best-remembered slogans of the war, 'Careless Talk Costs Lives', it produced a series of memorable posters. The public at large quickly accepted the principle behind the campaign and the slogan itself appeared on private notices like this one, as well as on the government's own publications.

Crews of British Ships,

BEWARE OF SPIES!

Don't talk about what you have done or are going to do. The enemy has ears everywhere.

Don't discuss Naval and Military affairs or the movements of ships or their cargoes or courses with strangers or foreigners

Don't trust anyone you do not know. ENEMY SPIES at home and abroad will try to draw you into arguments and entrap you into telling them about the movements of ships, their cargoes, the courses steered, and the steps taken to defend our ships.

Don't forget to report at once any person who tries to get information from you or from anyone else in your hearing.

Don't forget that your want of care may help the enemy, and lead to the loss of British ships and the deaths of their crews.

SECRECY MEANS SAFETY

W6104—68 75,000 7/17 HWV(P575)

Beware of Spies!, 1917

Spy scares were widespread in the United Kingdom on the outbreak of the First
World War, but very few reports and rumours turned out to be true. In the end,
eleven German spies were shot in the Tower of London, but the majority of claimed
sightings turned out to be figments of active imaginations. However, despite this, at
the height of the German submarine threat in 1917, the need for security was fully
justified. Vigilance was essential and discretion absolutely necessary.

LOOK OUT!

SABOTAGE

SCOTCH
THIS
by being

ALWAYS
ALERT

Report suspicious persons & things
AT ONCE

ISSUED BY LONDON PORT EMERGENCY COMMITTEE, AND PRINTED AT THE DOULTON PRESS, 73, MINORIES, E.C.3.

Look Out! Sabotage. London Port Emergency Committee

Security around ports is always difficult to maintain. Posters during the First World War had stressed the need for vigilance and discretion among merchant seamen. During the next war the same message was promoted again. The London Port Emergency Committee produced this poster, playing on latent concerns about enemy threats from within the community. In many ways the language is similar to 21st-century posters stressing the need for vigilance to combat the threat of terrorism.

STRIP TEASE

Private Nit-wit

Is the scrounger who, by 'winning' spares, tools and equipment, may lose battles. He stops repair of tanks, guns and lorries by R. A. O. C. Workshops. Every time he strips an evacuated vehicle he is helping the enemy

STOP HIM

he's dangerous !

2920/PMEE/5000 / 4-42

Strip Tease, 1942

Throughout the war, Britain's Ministry of Food and Ministry of Information used posters and their slogans as a dynamic weapon of war. Drawing on the talent of the pre-war advertising industry, the MOI engaged people through a combination of striking graphic design and ironic humour. Several successful campaigns centred around invented characters such as Potato Pete, Dr Carrot and Mrs Sew and Sew. Even the services adopted absurd characters such as Private Nit-wit to drive home their serious messages with a smile.

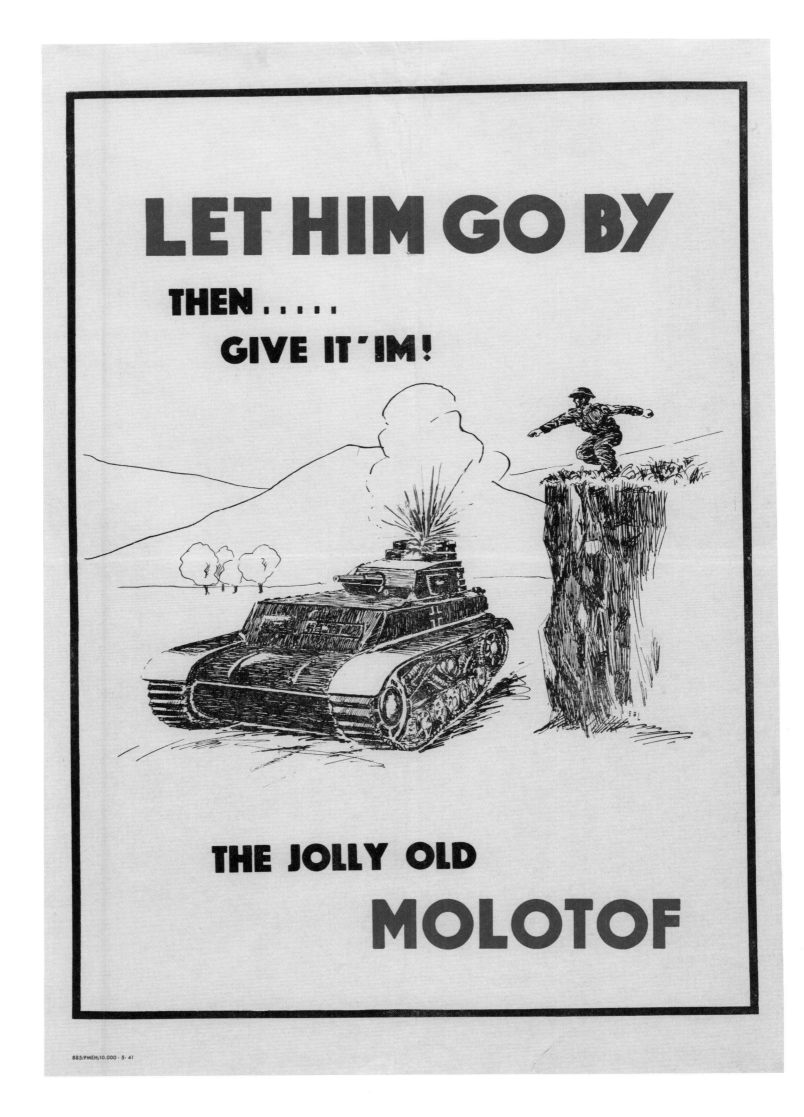

Let Him Go By, Then … Give It 'Im!, 1941

On 14 May 1940, following the German invasion of the Netherlands, the British government announced the formation of the Local Defence Volunteers. Some 250,000 men enrolled within the first twenty-four hours to defend their homeland, but lacking uniforms and equipment, the LDV had to arm themselves with makeshift weapons such as 'Molotov Cocktails' (petrol bombs). Many were experienced soldiers from the First World War. Recognizing the deeply patriotic foundations of the LDV, in August the Prime Minister, Winston Churchill, renamed it the more familiar 'Home Guard'.

Landing Craft
BRITISH AND AMERICAN

S. 1555.

L.C.P. (L)
LANDING CRAFT
PERSONNEL (LARGE)

L.C.P. (R)
LANDING CRAFT
(RAMPED)

L.C.A.
LANDING CRAFT ASSAULT

L.C.S. (M) Mk. I
LANDING CRAFT
SUPPORT (MEDIUM)

L.C.S. (L) Mk. I
LANDING CRAFT
SUPPORT (LARGE)

L.C.T. (5)
LANDING CRAFT
TANK

L.C.M. (1)
LANDING CRAFT
MECHANISED

L.C.T. (4)
LANDING CRAFT TANK

L.C.T. (3)
LANDING CRAFT TANK

L.C.M. (3)
LANDING CRAFT
MECHANISED

L.B.V. (2)
LANDING BARGE
VEHICLE Mk. 2

L.C.F. (3)
LANDING CRAFT FLAK
(THREE)

Landing Craft, British and American. Naval Intelligence Department

On 6 June 1944 Allied troops landed on the French coast of Normandy to begin the liberation of western Europe. In the first twenty-four hours, over 160,000 troops went ashore from more than 5,000 ships. Many of these were specialist landing craft that had been developed during the war to land both men and weapons. The larger vessels landed tanks and other armoured vehicles. Smaller ships transported the soldiers themselves. The Normandy landings were the largest amphibious operation ever undertaken.

Recognise Small Warships. Naval Intelligence Department

The rapid development during the Second World War of a whole arsenal of new
aircraft, ships and weapons meant that it was essential members of the armed forces
learnt which were on the Allied side and which belonged to the enemy. Books, charts,
posters and pocket guides were produced for soldiers, sailors and airmen. Civilians
too, including members of the Royal Observer Corps and thousands of school
children, also memorized the shapes of both friendly and hostile aircraft.

© IWM (PROC 008)

Nightshift Accuracy Helps the Night Ack Ack. Ministry of Supply

During the Second World War increasing numbers of women entered heavy industry.
By 1943, 600,000 women worked in engineering. Two-thirds of Rolls Royce's workforce
of 24,000 was female. At first the Amalgamated Engineering Union would not accept
women. But in time women's precision and skill were recognized and they were
allowed to join as members. It was seen that women could produce goods to the
same standards as men. However, despite this, women's pay remained significantly less.

© IWM (PROC 036)